The Mourne by Night

Fisherman Under Old Bridge

STRABANE

Rear View

Maureen Boyle

Strabane

photography by Malachi O'Doherty

Strabane

is published in 2020 by
ARLEN HOUSE
42 Grange Abbey Road
Baldoyle, Dublin 13, Ireland
Phone: 00 353 86 8360236
arlenhouse@gmail.com
arlenhouse.blogspot.com

Distributed internationally by
SYRACUSE UNIVERSITY PRESS
621 Skytop Road, Suite 110
Syracuse, NY 13244–5290
Phone: 315–443–5534
Fax: 315–443–5545
supress@syr.edu
syracuseuniversitypress.syr.edu

978–1–85132–221–3, *paperback*

Typesetting by Arlen House

Contents

The Mill, Sion

Photograph by Maureen Boyle

For Betty, Delma and Pat

Rock in River

Strabane

Windowsill

INTRODUCTION

This long poem *Strabane* was written as a commission by Overtone Productions for broadcast in the BBC Radio 4 series 'Conversations on a Bench'. Producer Anna Scott-Brown spent a week in Strabane – the border town in County Tyrone, Northern Ireland – recording conversations with local people about their lives in the town. Then poet Maureen Boyle, whose family are from the town and who grew up in Sion Mills, just outside it, used the recordings and her own childhood memories and family stories to write the poem. *Strabane,* read by the poet, was broadcast by BBC Radio 4 in December 2018 and January 2019.

The Mountain Beyond

I

This is my father's town,
An Srath Bán or 'the white shore'
from the bright pebbles
that the river carries here.

It was peopled first by friars,
saints' names survive around it
– Melmount, Ballycolman,
Urney for an oratory,
Camus-juxta-Mourne.

Settled first by Catholic Scots
before the Plantation proper,
the Hamiltons of Paisley
taking over the *Cúirt an Bhaird,*
the poet's seat at Baronscourt.

The Hamiltons became
the Dukes of Abercorn
who give their name to the square

that is not really a square
but still collecting groundrents
on the little buildings there.

Where Rivers Meet

II

Strabane is in a pocket of mountains
the river Mourne fed by the Sperrins –
Knocavoe, Bellcoo, Bessie Bell, Croghan –
names flowing down into the town
too for housing estates and parks.

And to the west the River Finn flows into it
at Lifford, its waters from the high hills
of Donegal, the gap at Barnesmore
which feeds the flow of river water
and of people

come in streams from Gweedore, Glenties,
Crolley, bringing the old language with them
and the *uaigneas* – the loneliness
of standing in this square to be hired,

most only children sleeping in barns
working for rich farmers,
many would stay and make their lives here,
my father's family from the island of Arranmore.

The Mill, Sion

Photograph by Maureen Boyle

III

Along the river and in Donegal
people grew flax in their fields –
the little blue flower growing well
in the river's wet beds that would rot and ret it for linen.

First they worked in their homes
and then the Herdmans came
to build a mill and a village –
a model English village by an Irish town.

My grandfather worked in the mill,
my mother vowed she never would,
seeing the sinister snow of scutched flax
that hid her father when she was sent
to bring him his lunch,
and made him wheeze
at night when he came home,
going out into the yard and burning
a circle of white powder
which he'd breath into his beleaguered lungs
to try to clear them –
one snow swapped for another,
a bowl by his bed to collect
the poison he'd cough up in the night.

Byssinosis, the price the workers paid
for the privilege of a wage and a tiny street house.

Fly Fisher

IV

The river was my grandfather's escape.
On the door of his dark, outside toilet
he'd hang the flies he tied with brightly-coloured thread.
Hair from squirrels' tails and badgers,
the breast feathers of the pheasant
would glint in the dark, tied Apache-style
– hackles turned to mimic the shrimp
or dragon fly, unlikely in a place we would dread.

He would lift small brown trout
and salmon grils from the Mourne
under the Swinging Bridge at Bearney,
the bridge my other grandfather had painted,
in places where the villagers still went in summers
to sunbathe and paddle at little pebble beaches
or sandy corners
knowing all the pools the fish liked and the weathers.

The weir intrigued us with its raging rush of water
near where the salmon leapt and a heron stood lonely
in wait of them – the weir's energy loud
beside the deathly-still depths of the Layde
that brought the water to the Mill
and where two little brothers drowned
one after the other in successive years –
their mother marked in what was left of life
by their shadowed loss.

The Layde

V

We were taught to fear the river for its dangers,
for river holes that were hidden and secret
but dared each other to cross the old railway bridge
that was rusted and gaping and long disused.

My father took me to travel on the last train
out of Sion Mills.
After he died I found he'd kept the ticket stump
and a photo shows my young father holding me
at the window as it left the station –
me plump in a knitted pixie hat.

Swinging Bridge

VI

Summer in Sion meant the tennis courts,
the Holm Field and cricket down the Mill Lane.
Long days playing in the fields by the railway lines
and in the sheep tunnels underneath, big spiders crawling
in the stones between the old sleepers,
cattle stinking in long grass.
In school Mrs Brady taught us to paint the trees
in each of their seasons –
the big chestnuts that lined the village streets
and the beech trees
whose mast we painted in bright colours in her class.

Lifford Bridge

VII

A counter current flowed above the river at Lifford
where the Mourne meets the Finn to form the Foyle.
Under the bridge salmon, trout, herons, kingfishers;
above, for years, miraculous cargoes
carried in pockets, bags, knickers and prams
an argosy of all that was rationed in the North
but available in the South:
chocolates, butter, sugar and shoes,
all you could wish for. My mother's pale buckskinned
Confirmation pumps ordered in Dooher's shop in Lifford,
sent from Dublin, then collected by her father
and smuggled across.

Lower Main Street, Rear

VIII

Strabane was a very old town to my child's eyes.
It smelled of coal fires and cooking fat.
We would be taken to the forge to watch the alchemy
of the farrier, to hear the music of metal and stare
into the black eyes of the horse that didn't flinch
as he held its foot to the fire.
We went there on Fridays for messages, and on Sundays
to Townhall Street for the Sunday papers after Mass.
Packie's shop was beside The Forresters' Hall
– the rehearsal rooms where the brass band practised –
the little oblong march cards
that attached to my father's clarinet by a lyre,
oddities yellowing on our piano for years.
Gentlemen then still wore three-piece black suits,
like my father's Uncle Charlie, the bandmaster,
who seemed a relic of Dickens,
a cross between Charlie Chaplin and Einstein
with his wonderful moustache,
the folds of his suit musty and rich, as he'd pull out
a handkerchief to snort snuff
or check his gold watch on a chain.

Chippy

IX

As we grew up it seemed glamorous!
My mother's cousins, one who shared my name,
visited in winter in their London mini-skirts
and took me and my sister shopping on a Saturday night
to Wrights' drapery with its long mirrors,
deep carpets and beautiful clothes,
then to Cassoni's for chips and coke floats.
There were taxis outside the Commercial Hotel,
rain on the streets, dark puddles lit by the shop windows
and 'Downtown' by Petula in our heads.

Melmount Cemetery

X

And then something came to blow the past away.
A curly-haired youth from Derry marched
into the old Town Hall,
the very heart of the town for two hundred years
where people went to dance on its well-sprung floor
and for theatre,
and said, 'Everyone out!'
leaving an absence in Ireland's name
that seems even now not to have filled.

In those days we'd hear a dull thump
in the distance and know another one
had gone off and wonder if anyone had died.
One day in school, they sent us home
via High Seein – the fairy mound –
to miss the bomb, and when the sound
came up the road we wondered what the target was
only to find, it was our friend's family's chip shop.

On the news, we heard stories of people
shot through their doors,
and when a traveller's car broke down
and he rang our bell in the night
I'd lie in bed willing my father not to respond,
imagining the figure on the other side
shooting through the glass.
We worried too on all the nights he did the census in '71
around the Plum and the television mast
when they said they'd shoot the census takers.

Abercorn Square I

Photograph by Maureen Boyle

Danny McLaughlin's shop was another target
when in the name of Ireland underpants and socks
would fly into the sky
and after each bomb – the sale in which
my father acquired gorgeous tweeds
from the Scottish islands and Donegal –
Harris, Mc Nutt's and Magee –
they would never truly lose the smell of smoke.
So that when you opened my parents' wardrobe for years
after there was that small trace of something dark
and my father smelling of a forest fire.

Snow

XI

One night in Frognal in Hampstead
when I had been years away
the name of the town was suddenly on the news;
three young men's faces
shot dead in a field at the head of the town
waiting to shoot the army.

And not long after
my English friend came back with me
and walking over the bridge
couldn't understand
why his countrymen with guns
treated him with suspicion
and asked where he was from
until he spoke and they heard
a voice from Doncaster.

Palimpsest

Photograph by Maureen Boyle

XII

Today, approached from the old bridge over the river,
the town stands like a huddle of herons
grey and hunched,
the old buildings open to the sky
and swoops of pigeons lighting on the rooves
roosting in the gaps among the buddleia
that sprout from unused chimney pots.
Ghost names of businesses that once thrived,
a palimpsest caught between the gables
– Harley's Drapers, Divine's Tea Merchants,
Smyth's Mills.

Harley's

Photograph by Maureen Boyle

XIII

How do the salmon know how to return?
They say the river's smells
imprints on the smolts
so that they know the very pebble bed they were born in
– not the river alone but its tributary.
And so they come back
year-after-year if they survive the ocean winters
swimming against the current,
the fresh water washing off silvery camouflage
that kept them safe in the sea,
taking on the browns and orange
of the river's peaty bed instead
until they are home to make another redd
and begin the cycle all over again.

The Heron by the Weir

Flies

Heron Waiting on the Weir

Acknowledgements

Thanks to Eilish Rooney who made the initial connection. To Overtone Productions – Anna Scott-Brown and Adam Fowler – for the invitation to do 'Conversations on a Bench' and to BBC Radio 4 for broadcasting it. Thanks to all who came to talk to Anna in August 2018 in Strabane: Gerard Bradley; Helen Campbell; Joe Cullen; June Egelund-Jenkins; Frank Elliot; Libby Hart; Celia Herdman; John Heaney; Michael Kennedy; Hugh Moss; Gloria Perry; Shirley Russell; Ann Speers. Special mention to Pat Gillespie who died a year after the conversation. I used Jim Bradley's book, *The Fair River Valley: Strabane Through the Ages,* edited by John Dooher and Michael Kennedy. Thanks also to my mother Betty for her help in suggesting good storytellers and contributing some stories herself!

Abercorn Square II

Photograph by Maureen Boyle

About the Illustrator

Photo by Lily Boyle

Malachi O'Doherty is a writer and broadcaster based in Belfast. His most recent book, *Fifty Years On: The Troubles and the Struggle for Change in Northern Ireland,* was published by Atlantic Press in 2019. Malachi is also known for his photography, both in his published books, exhibitions and on social media. His ninth book, a novel, will be published by Merrion Press in 2020. He is a recent recipient of a Major Artist Award from the Arts Council of Northern Ireland. He is married to Maureen Boyle.

Flann O'Brien on Abercorn Square

Photograph by Maureen Boyle

About the Author

Photo by Malachi O'Doherty

Maureen Boyle lives in Belfast. She began writing as a child in Sion Mills, County Tyrone, winning a UNESCO medal for a book of poems in 1979 at the age of eighteen. She studied in Trinity College, Dublin and did postgraduate work in the University of East Anglia, the University of Ulster and in 2005 was awarded a Masters in Creative Writing at Queen's University Belfast. She has won various awards including the Ireland Chair of Poetry Prize in 2007 and the Strokestown International Poetry Prize in the same year. In 2013 she won the Fish Short Memoir Prize. She has received support from the Arts Council of Northern Ireland in the form of Individual Arts, ACES and Travel Awards. In 2008 she was commissioned to write a poem on the Crown Bar in Belfast for a BBC documentary. A limited edition pamphlet appeared in June 2019 of her poem 'The Nunwell Letter' written for the inaugural Ireland Chair of Poetry Travel Bursary awarded in 2017 to research John Donne's wife, Ann More's stay on the Isle of Wight in 1611. Some of her work has been translated into German. She taught Creative Writing with the Open University for ten years and teaches English in St Dominic's Grammar School in Belfast. *The Work of a Winter*, her debut collection of poetry, was launched in December 2017, and is currently in its second edition. The collection was shortlisted for the 2019 Shine/Strong Award.

Island in the River